KELLY HOPPEN

CLOSE UP

QUADRILLE

Text by Helen Chislett　　　**Photography** by Thomas Stewart

KELLY HOPPEN

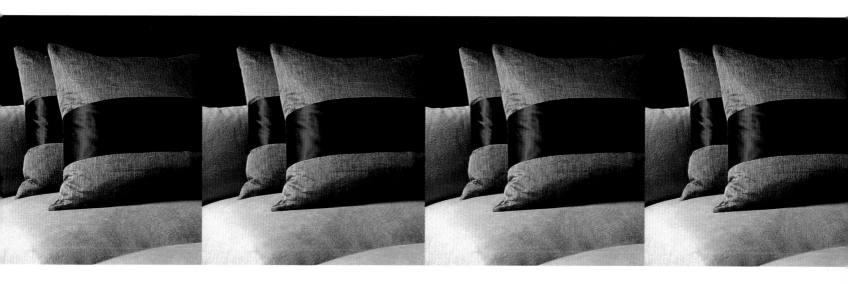

CLOSE UP

ATTENTION TO DETAIL IN DESIGN

to friends

CONTENTS

FOREWORD

The idea of producing a book that zooms in close, rather than taking the conventional broad picture, was an exciting concept to me. Firstly, it reflects my own philosophy that each view within a room, no matter how small, is important. Often it is not the big decisions that make the difference between mediocre and superlative design, but the attention to detailing. Choosing an upholstery material, for example, is only the beginning when dressing a chair. Thinking about stitching, piping, introducing textural contrast through cushions or deciding on the perfect backdrop is what transforms that chair into a focal point.

I also wanted to convey the sense of movement in a room; the fact that an interior is not static. It is human nature to become bored, be it with our clothes or our homes. It may not be practical to redecorate every few months, but it is possible to regenerate a space by moving, exchanging or altering some components within it. Close Up is full of such ideas. It shows you how to look at a room and really see it; how to focus on each individual object; and how to keep a space alive and organic.

I have enjoyed working on this book more than I could ever have envisaged, partly because putting my style under a magnifying lens has given me a different perspective on my work. The pictures are a joy, but do find time to read the text as well because it is like a bridge between what the eye sees and how the mind plans. There are no rules here. What I hope is that by showing you how I work, you can take my ideas and translate them into your own decorative style. Anything goes: the rarely admitted secret of decorating is that anything will work if it works for you. The integral part of design is understanding who you are and how you want to live.

This book is a gift from me to you. May it bring you much pleasure.

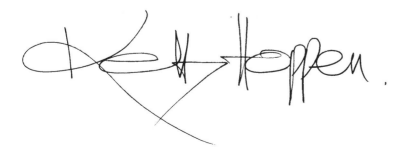

THE KELLY HOPPEN SIGNATURE

This book – a look through the zoom lens at what I do – provides a perfect opportunity to explain what my work is all about. Magazines and newspapers often dub me a minimalist. In fact, although I admire the minimalists and have learnt a great deal from them – the way in which they interpret a space is cleaner and clearer than anybody's – I am not, and never have been, a minimalist. My own style is actually warm rather than stark, luxurious rather than ascetic and organic rather than static. I like to begin with a space that is very structured and edited, but then to inject it with warmth and comfort. The unexpected way I juxtapose textures, objects or shapes within a room underpins much of what I do, but would be interpreted by a true minimalist as positively frivolous. Whereas a minimalist keeps the lines of a room etched sharply across a space, I like to begin with those same lines but then blur them at the edges.

When designing, I work on instinct alone – never really stopping to think about why something works or how a room comes together. This book is an invitation to step inside my head and to see what I see when I look at an interior. Space is obviously the first consideration, but many people think of a space as something to be filled. I believe that first you have to understand the space – its physical properties, the strength and direction of light within it and its interplay with adjacent spaces. It is also essential to relate it to the people who will be using it and how they will be using it.

When it comes to positioning furniture and other objects within a space, it is important not to fill it so tightly that movement is restricted. That word, movement, relates not just to being able to walk around in comfort, but also to movement of the eye. Allowing a certain amount of space between individual items gives a room a sense of flow, which is calming. Don't punctuate the space with too many ingredients or it will have the awkwardness of a badly composed sentence.

The way I assemble a room in my head is by imagining it on a three-dimensional grid system. Structure is crucial to my work, so this linear interpretation of how a space works is invaluable. However, it also overflows into other aspects of my design life: runners, rows, banding or panels also stress this geometric approach, a way of imposing order onto previously disharmonious interiors.

However, once the core design is in place, my natural tendency is to look for ways of shaking it up. A room that is over-disciplined is in danger of becoming boring, so I like to introduce a touch of excitement –

something contrived to catch the eye. This is quite a subtle technique: it would be completely against my philosophy to introduce anything garish or vulgar just for the sake of it. It might be that I place a very small-scaled object adjacent to a large one; a group of identical, symmetrically placed items alongside one asymmetrical piece; or, perhaps, a free, organic shape against a rigid man-made one. Texture also offers wonderful opportunities to make these visual plays. The mix of matt and glossy, rough and smooth, clear and opaque all contributes to the visual success of a room. Teaming a very humble fabric, such as felt or towelling, with something lavish, such as silk or taffeta, is a particularly pleasing way of overlaying that sense of interest.

I am absolutely passionate about detail. Everything I introduce into a room must have a sense of harmony. To me, it makes no sense at all to redecorate or refurnish a room and then ignore the way the cushions are stacked, flowers arranged or objects displayed. All the time that I am contemplating such details, I am considering them on two levels: the individual vista I am creating and then how that relates to the backdrop of the room itself. Nothing should be overlooked, whether it is the way sweets are arranged on a dish or photographs on a shelf.

I am also driven by a desire to bring atmosphere and mood into a home. Good artificial lighting is obviously a key component here, but so are scent, taste, music and touch. A home should wrap itself around you, so you feel completely warm, safe and cocooned. It is not enough that it looks fabulous: it must feel wonderful, too. Remember also that although a home should be a sanctuary, it is never isolated from the environment outside. A strong influence in achieving visual and tactile comfort lies in reflecting what is happening in the seasons. The grey days of winter need a different treatment from the airiness of summer or the sharpness of spring.

Finally, much of what I do is about stepping out of the ordinary. People assume that everything I use must be expensive. In fact, I love taking modest household objects and transforming them into chic additions to a home, with a little bit of lateral thinking. Baking trays, mixing bowls and lids of boxes are just a few of the examples you will find here. But remember that everything shown is intended to be a springboard for your own ideas. Once you have had a chance to look at my signature, it is time to think about creating one of your own.

ABOVE Even the smallest of objects can be arranged with care to add a layer of beauty to a room. Here, the opaque milky surface of eggs has been highlighted by a black lacquer plate. This allows one texture to play against another and is also an example of how the repetition of simple forms can create a still-life composition.

OPPOSITE Consider, too, the backdrop to an arrangement. Here, ornate creamy marble has been enhanced with a contemporary runner of polished plaster. The use of small-scale items – three ceramic bowls – adds an unexpected twist to a traditional fireplace. Their asymmetrical positioning also draws the eye, instead of allowing it to rest more conventionally at the centre of the mantelpiece.

RIGHT Rooms should never be designed in isolation, but should relate to those around them. Here the view from the dining room looks through to the hallway, where three tall wenge tables have been placed alongside each other to replicate a conventional console. Twists of tightly packed snake grass in round glass bowls on each one emphasise their height. Wenge has also been chosen for the dining table, with dark-edged picture frames above echoing its tones.

PAGE 16 One fabulously textured object can create a focal point within a room. This carved wooden artefact has a fascinating ridged surface which contrasts perfectly with the simple glass bowl and velvety chocolate cosmos.

PAGE 17 Fabric is another way of bringing a textural highlight to a room. This pleated, chocolate Fortuny silk flows to the floor as if it were liquid. Dark-stained floorboards create a dramatic backdrop.

PAGE 18 The same fabric can now be seen in full, used to cover a hallway chair. Behind is a striking black-and-white photograph of Glenn Close, which has been positioned to create impact as visitors walk in.

PAGE 19 Rooms should taste as delicious as they look. Feed the senses by displaying food seductively. Here, a silver dish on an antique Chinese table makes the perfect foil for chocolate-covered coffee beans.

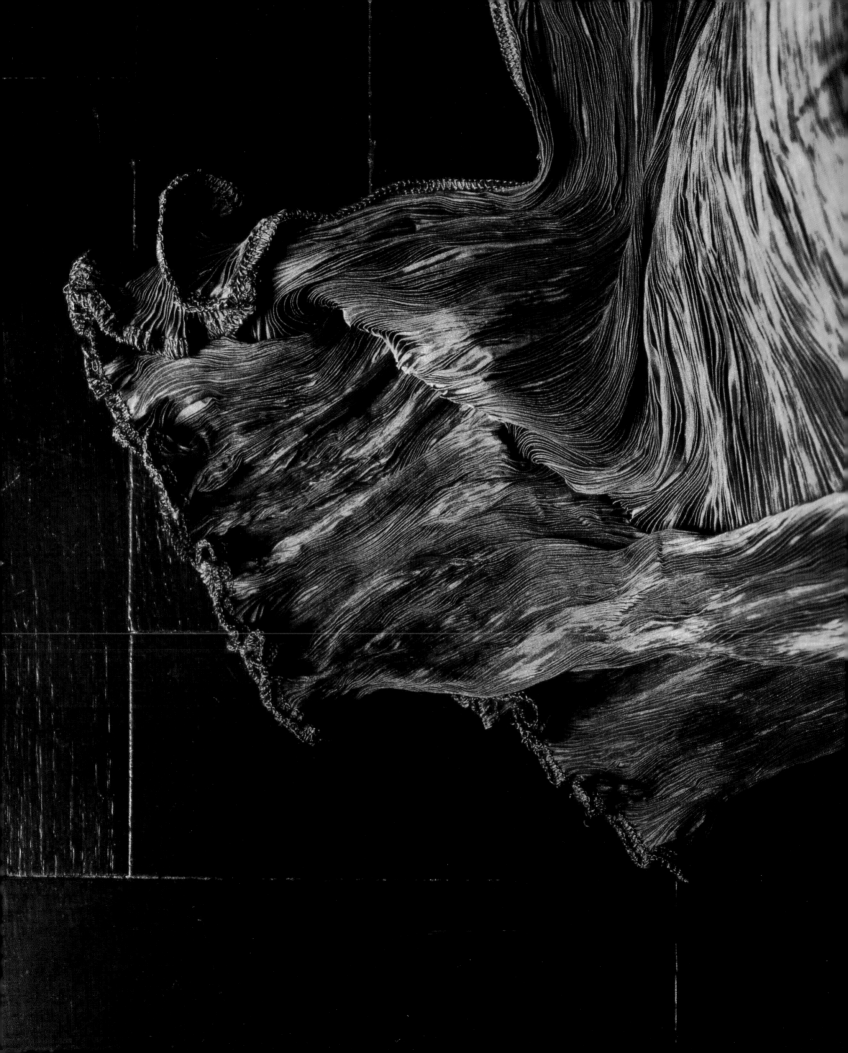

SPACES SEEN AND UNSEEN

The golden rule I always try to make people understand is that to transform your home you must be able to see not only objects but the space between objects. A space, to me, is as important visually as a fabric or a table. It is part of the balance of the room and must be considered on an aesthetic level.

As with anything else, it can be analysed on varying scales. If you are designing a whole room, it is best to empty it of everything so you can rub out your mental picture of it. Think about its shape, proportions and architecture. Note the position of doors, windows and fireplace. Now try mentally to dissolve the walls, so you can see how this room leads into other spaces within the house and how each space relates to the next. Do not rush this process. Spend as much time as you need simply looking and contemplating. Play music that you love and allow yourself to become immersed in your thoughts. The idea is to expand your mind so that you can see all the possibilities for a room, rather than becoming entrenched in how it is now.

The beauty of learning to look at space is that this technique can be applied to small cameos as well as large areas. Perhaps this is not the moment to redecorate on a grand scale. Instead it might be that you want to revitalise your home, rather than completely transform it. Concentrating on creating pleasing still lifes around a room can train the eye just as effectively.

Decide on the corner you want to rejuvenate, such as a mantelpiece, side table or alcove. Empty it – no matter how much you love the objects usually displayed. Pack everything in boxes and put them out of sight for at least six months. They will make a reappearance in your life at some point in the future, but nothing should remain static – least of all a home.

Now consider that area in terms of colour, texture and lighting. These are the means by which you are going to make a canvas on which to paint, metaphorically speaking. Look at the textures that are there, such as the smoothness of marble or the richness of wood. Now think how you might emphasise these qualities by introducing objects with a contrasting surface. Once you have found your inspiration, it might be a question of using items you already own but placing them in a new setting, or buying something with this space specifically in mind. However, when positioning them, remember to keep looking at the space as well as at what you are putting into it. Be critical: take as long as you wish to move things around, introducing or discarding certain elements until you have created something that is in balance with its surroundings.

The more you concentrate on the small vistas of a room, the easier it becomes to change the bigger picture.

You must also have an awareness of the importance of spaces never usually seen: the insides of cupboards and drawers, for example. Order is so important to our mental wellbeing that it is not enough merely to pay it lip service by applying it to what is on display. It should be evident throughout an interior – and that includes those seldom-seen places. Opening a cutlery drawer to find everything immaculately stored and ready for use is just as uplifting as opening a door to find a room arranged with care and intelligence.

When looking at the space as a whole, you should first reflect on its physical boundaries. You also need to develop an awareness of the natural light. Work with the light you have, before making decisions about incorporating artificial lighting. If you were building a house on a plot of land, the first thing you would do is calculate where the sun rises and sets. That in turn would help you to decide on the position and outlook of rooms. In a house that is already built, you still need to know how light falls at different times of the day and the year. How else will you know where best to position furniture? Just as the space between objects is as important as the objects themselves, so shadows are as beautiful as light. Once you know how light moves, you can decide whether you want it to flow into the room uninterrupted or would like to filter it or diffuse it in order to create interesting effects of light and dark. It is not until you have fully comprehended the natural light in your home that you can make decisions about the artificial kind. The latter is not only for use by night. It can also boost grey days, throw attention onto a particular tableau or become a decorative form in its own right.

The room may still be empty, but now you must imagine filling it with furniture, objects and textures. Don't lose sight of the space itself. Remember, this is as important as all the decorative items you plan to introduce. Once you have an image in your mind, you could transfer these thoughts to a story board. Create a montage of inspirational pictures, colour samples, fabric swatches and sketches to show you how the room would look.

Now is the time for a moment of honesty. Does the picture you have created correspond to the type of person you are? Do you have the discipline not only to create the look, but to live in it? This is not a showpiece, but your home. You have to feel comfortable with it, just as you have to feel at ease in the clothes you wear or the car you drive. Think about how you live and the people who live with you. Lifestyle is the most important ingredient and it must be at one with the space.

ABOVE AND OPPOSITE The dining room seen on pages 14–15 has now been laid for dinner. Although the basic components of wenge table and Alcantara-covered chairs remain unchanged, a transformation has been achieved through linen, tableware and accessories. The picture opposite shows a bird's-eye view of the place settings with taupe, deep purple and lilac plates combining to produce a mood conducive to nocturnal dining. Wine glasses are also pale amethyst. Taupe linen napkins and a linen runner placed along the length of the table create a visual link to the chairs and the curtains behind. Silver glasses placed centrally in a row are the perfect containers for tea lights, which create a soft glow in keeping with the subdued colour scheme.

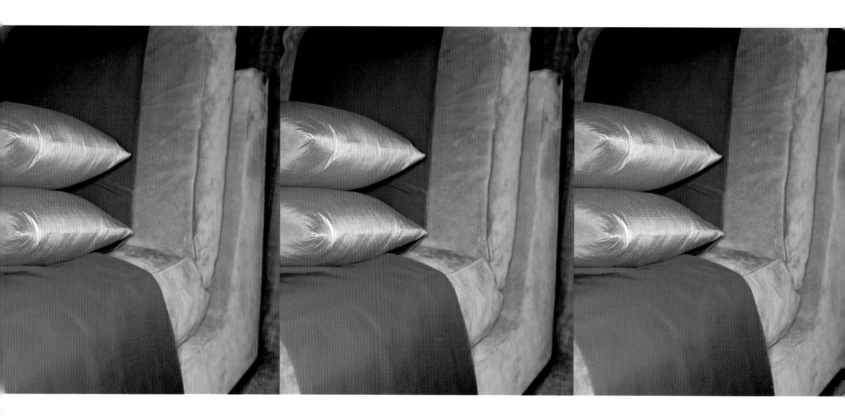

ABOVE It is not necessary when decorating to lavish money on every item, but it does create an impact if you choose one or two objects to turn into eye-catching focal points. These antique chairs from Paris are covered in lush suede and have been further enhanced by purple silk runners and silk cushions. The result is luxurious and seductive, an invitation to relax into a cocoon of opulent fabrics.

OPPOSITE A completely different space for day or night can be created by using walls that are fluid rather than solid. Here, runners of different fabrics – sheers, silks, even leather – are hung the height of the room and can be changed according to the desired mood. Used by night, as shown here, they create a dramatic setting for a dinner party. Rich purple glasses, a satin runner, glass plates and napkins made of three different silks combine to give a backdrop to a Bacchanalian feast.

OPPOSITE PAGE A close-up of the dining room shown previously focuses the eye on the raw silk of the dining chairs and the way in which this blends with the banner-style runners hung along the walls. This use of fabric emphasises the soft boundaries of the room and creates an atmosphere that is truly inviting.

BELOW LEFT The classic lines of this Mies van der Rohe stool have been emphasised by the soft swathe of a cashmere throw. This makes an interesting contrast to the curved stainless steel legs and white leather upholstery. A coir floor adds a further textural dimension.

ABOVE RIGHT The shape of a wenge-inserted panel in a row of bedroom cupboards has been echoed here by the positioning of two cotton runners over a mohair bedspread, with appliquéd satin rectangles. The linen cushions continue the geometric theme with appliquéd satin squares.

ABOVE Taupe suede has been combined with dark green wool to create a smart Roman blind for a dressing room. The sheen of the tortoiseshell box makes a pleasing contrast to the matt of the suede. Three tall jars filled with curling iris leaves make an unexpected departure from a conventional floral arrangement.

OPPOSITE Touches of colour can be used to create subtle visual links within a room, pulling the eye from place to place. Here, the red wool of the cushion on a suede chair echoes that of the mango arum lily in the glass bowl. Twines of pussy willow also pick out the wenge-and-ivory of the lamp set behind the wenge table.

OPPOSITE Texture is also an effective way of bringing all the strands in a scheme together. This bird's-eye view looks down on a wooden floor and silk carpet bound with chocolate-brown leather. Leather has also been chosen for the chair upholstery and as a band over the linen back cushion. A small chocolate-brown ostrich cushion finishes off the composition to spectacular effect.

ABOVE An upright view of the same chair shows how each ingredient balances with the others. Set against wenge shelving filled with books, it creates a quiet area within the room. The positioning of books has been given the same consideration as that of any other object – note how they have been assembled according to scale, proportion and colour. Fibre optic lighting set into the unit edges adds interest without disturbing the tranquil mood.

This elegant living room has been arranged so that the shape of each object interplays with those around it. Note how the horizontal line of the wooden coffee table is echoed by the slats of the seat back, or how the pedestal table in the background has a scaled-down reflection in the lamp on the floor. The dark wenge of the chair has been complemented by rich red leather upholstery and a sumptuous red horsehair cushion. Textural harmony continues with the bound linen rug and linen curtains. A collection of amethyst-coloured glass on the table makes the perfect backdrop for fiery red clove carnations, a jolt of colour in a monochrome room.

32

Viewed from a different angle, it is now possible to see that the living room is in fact on mezzanine level and looks down onto the dining room shown on page 25. Here you can see the full impact of ceiling-to-floor panels in linen and leather viewed over the balcony of toughened glass. These vertical lines have a strong influence on the scheme and are picked out throughout the room. The wenge chair with horsehair cushion is now seen face on, providing a link to the wenge lights and tables behind. The whole composition is extremely sophisticated, right down to the glass balustrades of the staircase, the Chinese lacquer boxes and the Kelly Hoppen rugs.

OPPOSITE A close-up of one of the Kelly Hoppen rugs shown on the previous page, with the distressed lacquer coffee table and parquet floor, illustrates how strong linear pattern is within a scheme. Using two contrasting colours – red and black – emphasises their graphic quality.

ABOVE The cube shapes of sugary Turkish delight have been echoed here by a geometric arrangement on a slab of square slate. The spaces between each one have been considered as carefully as those of a permanent still life within a room.

SYMMETRY AND ASYMMETRY

Because the linear dimension is so important to me, it is natural to embrace symmetry in design. Symmetry impresses order onto a space and that is something I value very much. Just as understanding space is a question of seeing the space between objects, so arranging an interior is about recognising the relationship between objects. Form, scale, texture and colour all give clues as to how best to achieve harmony in a scheme.

At its most obvious, symmetry is about taking two or more identical objects and placing them close to each other for maximum visual impact. It is one of the unfailing techniques of decorating and is apparent in interiors ranging from English country houses to New York loft spaces. However, it has other interpretations, too, such as repeating a shape in different scales. This could include, for example, different-sized cushions layered one onto the other, or a collection of identical vases ranging from low to high. Although this is not symmetry in its strictest sense, it has the same effect in an interior of emphasising structure and form. Finally, it can be about arranging furniture and objects in a symmetrical manner. This might be achieved through the way chairs and tables are positioned, how pictures are hung, the arrangements on shelves or mantelpieces, or through very geometrical window treatments. It can be achieved through the juxtaposition of perfectly balanced objects or by teaming up objects that, although not identical, have corresponding qualities which link them together. It might be the way a painting echoes the shape of a fireplace, for example, or how a lampshade reflects the form of a cabinet.

Whatever the approach, for symmetry to retain its force everything in a room must be carefully edited. If there is too much going on in terms of colour, pattern or extraneous objects, the eye will be distracted. Instead, you must strive to be as disciplined as possible about what is on display, so that attention is naturally focused on the intended area.

Whereas symmetry is fairly easily understood, asymmetry is often overlooked. An asymmetrical arrangement might include one object that bears no obvious relation to those surrounding it. It might, on the other hand, include identical objects that are positioned in an asymmetrical way. Like symmetry, it is a powerful instrument in design, particularly when used in conjunction with a symmetrical arrangement. The stark contrast between one and the other is a way of throwing each into sharp relief. If you find this hard to comprehend, consider how textures are used in interiors. If you choose something rich for a curtain, such as silk, there is little point in teaming it with something equally opulent – taffeta, say – because the textures will merge together. Instead you might choose to put silk with something humble, such as scrim or felt. The contrast will delight the eye and sense of touch, and will allow both to be appreciated fully.

So it is with symmetry and asymmetry. Start with your symmetrical arrangement and then place something close to it off centre. This will punctuate the space and inject some excitement into the design. It might be a question of using one tall object, so that height becomes a factor. It might be that you introduce an organic shape against a line of regimented ones. It could be that instead of hanging pictures in rows, you lean them against a wall with each frame overlapping.

Carry this idea one step further by thinking about how you might arrange identical objects in an asymmetrical way. Take a mantelpiece arrangement as an example. The traditional way of dressing one is to have a centrepiece of some description – perhaps a clock – and then to lead out from each side of this with symmetrical arrangements of candlesticks, photo frames, lamps, vases of flowers or ornaments, or any other decorative extras. But let us say you placed a pair of lamps at one end of the mantel and a clay figure at the other, with nothing else between but a simple row of single banana leaves in tumblers, each positioned to point in the same direction. Attention would still be drawn to the clay figure, even though it is not centre stage or surrounded by symmetry. In fact this would be a far more dynamic arrangement than the conventional sort, because symmetry and asymmetry would be working together to achieve something unpredictable and visually stimulating.

This is important, because good design is about avoiding the obvious. Just as combining textures is about finding contrast, so arranging objects is about considering the conventional treatment first and then looking for ways to turn this on its head. Remember this next time you are creating a still life of objects, be it on open shelves, a side table, a mantelpiece or in an alcove. It is not that success is guaranteed – be prepared for several attempts before finding the one you like – but that taking a fresh eye to any situation is a way of engendering inspiration. Once you begin to analyse the qualities that symmetry and asymmetry bring to a room, you will have fun discovering what powerful tools they can be.

OPPOSITE When considering each view within a room, think carefully about how every object affects those around it. The organic shape of this Arne Jacobsen chair makes an interesting play against the rigidity of a floating shelf. The symmetry of three identical glass vases, each holding a single-stem red dahlia, is reduced by placing them asymmetrically at one end of the shelf. Overlapping photo frames in different sizes also place symmetry and asymmetry in tandem and contribute to the balance of the total effect.

ABOVE Consider the vertical dimension as well when creating interesting vistas. The elongated light hung above this Perspex table is an unexpected contrast to the broadness of the Vietnamese lacquer vase filled with Bordeaux dahlias. The vibrant red of these is picked out in the red velvet runner placed over the table, bringing an exciting rush of colour to an otherwise calm scheme.

ABOVE LEFT A bed is like a canvas on which you can paint colours and textures. Here, an ostrich bedhead is complemented by crisp white linen, a red velvet runner, Chinese rattan head rests, a striped silk long cushion and a satin eiderdown. The result is a blend of wonderful textural contrasts and a perfectly balanced composition.

ABOVE RIGHT A separate view of the room featured on page 32 shows the wenge chairs on one side of the room and the creamy velvet upholstery on the other. Red cushions on each act as a visual bridge, with dark glassware and crimson flowers punctuating the space.

OPPOSITE A close-up of the wenge chair shows the printed red leather upholstery and horsehair cushion which bring a layer of richness to the scheme. Even one fabulous texture, such as the horsehair, can be enough to bring a whole room to life.

OPPOSITE Objects work particularly well when arranged in groups of three, five or seven; often even numbers result in an over-symmetrical format. Here wooden cylinders from Africa create an unusual still life, with a single cocoa leaf for impact. The rough concrete floor is a good foil to the richness of the wood.

PAGE 44 Collections of non-identical but similar objects also work well visually. Here, shagreen boxes of different sizes create a pleasing still life against an antique mirror. Reflected in this is a French *chaise-longue* and sculptural light, while in the foreground a silver bottle laid over the boxes adds a further decorative touch.

PAGE 45 Cushions of different sizes look particularly appealing when made of varying textures but similar colours. Here Alcantara suedes, velvets and silks in various finishes complement each other, while contrasting well with the textured wall behind.

OPPOSITE This perfectly harmonised composition draws together the key components of height, scale, texture and interest. The wenge cabinet and leather light set the style, but it is the sculptural shape of papyrus in a vase lined with cocoa leaves, juxtaposed with the unusual subject matter of the photograph, that determines the mood. The inclusion of small objects emphasises the large scale of the vase, while two pencils have been placed in the horn beaker to reflect the number of ceramic bowls close by.

ABOVE This cool living room illustrates the beauty of the monochrome scheme. The dark-stained wooden floor has been balanced by a simple cream rug bordered with leather. A tall wenge light and wenge sofa base echo the floor tones, but the linen shade, pale-coloured upholstery and sheer curtains act as a foil to these. Instead of a conventional coffee table, a banquette has been used. This can double as additional seating or be used as a surface for trays of drinks or flowers, such as the green papyrus shown here. Cushions in suede, linen and leather are stacked to emphasise the ordered atmosphere.

OPPOSITE The colours and textures of food can be key players in creating a delicious still life. Here vegetable crisps have been placed in a wooden bowl, which catches the light around its rim.

ABOVE In this dining area of a kitchen, a wenge table has been teamed with banquette seating and chocolate-brown chairs, all upholstered in linen with a plastic finish so that they can be wiped clean easily. Sticks of snake grass cut to fit the dimensions of a wooden bowl are a simple but effective centrepiece, while others have been placed in simple glass vases just behind the banquette. An old kitchen clock adds character.

GRIDS AND LINES

Designing a room can be either a fairly organic process or a very structured one. While I love organic shapes, I believe in underlying structure. Every room I work on translates itself into my head as a grid system, on which ideas then take shape.

Look around the room you are in now. Having practised mentally removing everything and concentrating only on the space itself, now try to imagine it is dissected by crisscrossing lines – not only from side to side, but up to down. You may find this easier to do if you draw up a scaled floor plan on graph paper, but it is important to take three dimensions into account, not just two. Mentally, this may be challenging at first, but persevere until the lines in your head are as real as if they were painted through the air. These grids will guide you not only when it comes to choosing the right scale of furniture for a room, but in understanding how each object relates to the next in terms of scale and form.

Extend this grid into adjacent rooms, so that you become increasingly aware of vistas through doorways. Think about how internal architecture, such as windows and fireplaces, creates squares that fit into the grid. Can these be echoed through blinds or mirrors, perhaps? Imagine the floor with lines leading off it at all sides. Use this vision to position furniture, rugs or other objects.

Even if you find it hard to see a room in this way, you can still use linear elements to impose structure on a space. Runners, for example, have become an integral part of design for me. I was first inspired to use them by visiting Japan and studying the way kimonos fold, forming a runner effect down the back. Straight lines delight me because I strive for order and balance in my interiors. It seemed I had found a way of achieving just that through strips of fabric that could be used down tables, on the backs of chairs, wrapped around cushions or banded onto curtains. The more I used them, the more I found ways to use them: as specialist paint effects, on bedheads, as rugs or on room dividers.

Once you begin to play with something in this way, you realise its limitless potential. Now I use runners and banding not only to emphasise structure, but also to introduce a change of texture or colour into a scheme according to mood or season.

Rows are another simple way of emphasising the linear. A line of identical objects, be they large or small, creates a focal point while also making a strong visual link to the overall layout of the room.

Working on a grid system might imply a rigidity of thought that is at odds with true creativity. It should be emphasised, then, that although design might have a solid central structure, it should always be overlaid with other elements that are free and organic. That is what gives interiors their excitement: the idea that something wild is imposed onto something disciplined. But this is truly effective only when the structure is in place first.

This approach will eventually permeate every decision you make concerning your home. Once you begin to analyse spaces in terms of grids and lines, considering carefully how each ingredient fits with the next, you will no longer be tempted to buy something on impulse and expect it to fit in. It will result in a more considered way of choosing furniture and furnishings. Rooms can so easily be unbalanced by an ill-judged addition; better to edit a room vigorously, then fill it slowly, really thinking about where each item should go.

If you want to gain confidence when it comes to applying grid systems to interiors, begin with a fairly modest project. Rather than trying to deconstruct an entire room in this way, think about how you might lay a square or rectangular table for dinner. The table provides the area on which you work. It is like a room in this sense. An undercloth can then be used to create a backdrop for everything else that is to be introduced. Runners of coordinating fabric can either be used lengthways to accentuate the existing proportions, or be placed horizontally to trick the eye into believing the table to be wider than it actually is. Runners placed in both directions create their own grid effect.

The chairs around the table should not be overlooked. Runners hung down their backs not only give them added interest, but tie them visually to the table itself. Plates, glasses and cutlery will naturally be positioned in a linear arrangement, which will echo the runner down the length of the table. This sense of order can be further emphasised by rows of candles or flowers down the centre of the table. Before the look becomes too uniform, blur the edges with table linen that can be swathed over plates.

There are many variations on this particular theme, but the secret is to understand how each element interplays with the next. Dressing the dining table is not just about creating atmosphere, but can encourage you to look at a room in a completely different way. The lessons applied here can be interpreted just as easily in the way a mantelpiece is arranged or open shelving is filled. It can even be the first step to designing a room in a truly architectural fashion.

ABOVE One of the most enjoyable aspects of design is to take a conventional idea and give it a twist. Here, for example, rather than using one large mirror above a wenge console table, a pair of wenge-framed mirrors have been used. These in turn reflect the wenge cabinets at the other end of the room. The graphic lines of this arrangement have been emphasised by the symmetrically placed pair of lamps and the collection of silver teapots in gradations of scale.

OPPOSITE A close-up of one wenge cabinet shows how a similar subtle change of scale has been used to draw attention to the individual Moroccan ceramic bowls displayed here. Cleverly designed lighting within adds a further layer of interest and is enhanced by the wenge light to the right. The pale-coloured shade of this echoes the creaminess of the china.

ABOVE Here the mirror over the fireplace is a contemporary interpretation of a traditional juxtaposition. It is as though the fireplace had a removable central panel which has been lifted out and placed above, so exactly does one shape fit into the other. The square table echoes this effect, while antique amethyst-coloured rummers are set off centre to blur the rigidity of the lines.

BELOW Cushions with geometric panels and borders impose a sense of order upon surroundings. Here they emphasise the form of the bedhead, which is upholstered in ox blood and camel cotton.

OPPOSITE Fibre optic lighting on the edges of open shelves is a clever way of giving definition to a quiet area.

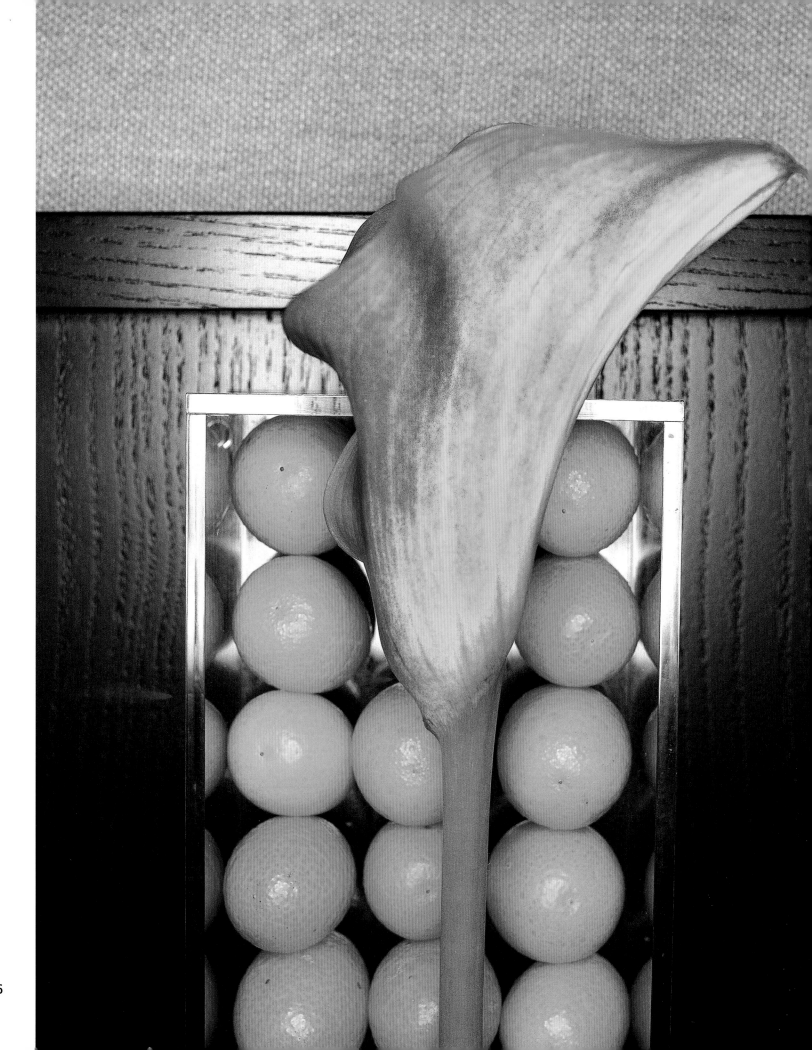

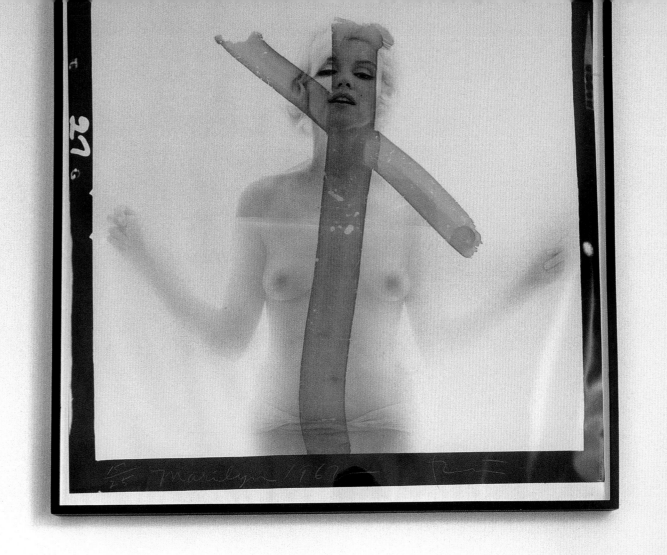

OPPOSITE A different view of the living room shown on page 47 demonstrates how the introduction of one strong colour can alter the mood of a room. Here an orange pashmina makes a luxurious throw or can be used as a band around a cushion. Replacing the green papyrus with an arrangement of kumquats emphasises this dynamic effect.

ABOVE Long loaves of bread are tied with rope for added textural definition. Placed on a simple polished concrete table against a limestone floor, they make an unusual still life.

PAGE 56 A bird's-eye view of the kumquats seen opposite shows them laid in a Perspex box, placed on a wooden tray on the linen banquette. The one spectacular mango arum lily laid on top not only accentuates the power of the colour, but creates an interesting asymmetrical effect against the carefully arranged rows of fruit.

PAGE 57 Choose pictures that complement the scale of their surroundings. This striking photograph of Marilyn Monroe is a strong image which perfectly combines with the very graphic modern fireplace. The orange cross scratched over the image adds another layer of interest to a bedroom that is otherwise monochrome.

PAGE 60 Scale is a key player in this contemporary bedroom. The huge mirror leaning against the wall matches the scale of the door. In its reflection can be seen a wenge panel and cupboard doors. The shape of the television adds to the graphic strength of the room. On the floor, the organic shape of two ceramic eggs throws the angular arrangement into relief.

PAGE 61 Black picture frames are complemented here by wenge rails on which to hang clothes.

PAGE 62 When used as a group of three, these tall wenge tables replicate a traditional console in a hallway. Tightly packed bunches of snake grass in glass bowls emphasise their vertical lines.

PAGE 63 Rows of identical objects are an effective way of accentuating the linear; here Perspex boxes of moss in white sand displayed on a linen runner create an unusual alternative to a conventional floral arrangement.

SEASONAL LIVING

For those of us who live in places where the seasons roll on it is important to design homes that can reflect the altered state between summer and winter. The idea of dressing a house seasonally is not a new one, but it is true to say it is increasing in popularity as people become more confident about creating homes that really work for them. Although it is relevant from a visual point of view, more importantly it is a very practical thing to do. Your home should make you feel comfortable at all times. Part of that comfort is not feeling too hot or too cold, and this comes down to more than installing the correct heating system. It is about what floors feel like underfoot, whether upholstery fabrics are pleasant to the touch and how much light there is in a room. Different things make us feel comfortable at different times of the year; that is what seasonal decorating is concerned with and why it should be thought about on many levels.

If you keep colours minimal, it is possible to ring the changes through more subtle textural variations. First, consider window treatments. If privacy is not an issue, you may need neither curtains nor blinds at the height of summer. If you do want some protection from the outside world, think of gossamer-light sheers or semi-translucent unlined curtains. In winter, you may need something to prevent the cold air from outside circulating through your home, but this can be achieved easily with shutters or double glazing. It is not necessary to hang extra-thick curtains, which will allow in even less light than usual. The Shoji panels I designed for Silent Gliss were inspired by my own need to pay homage to the change in seasonal light, without sacrificing the feel-good factor in my own home. Now I can transform my interiors by hanging leather or linen one day, suede or scrim the next. I have even included a Perspex variation for a truly purist approach. Not only do the panels make excellent window treatments, but they can also be used as room dividers.

Thinking about how the windows are dressed is only the start. Probably the most important consideration is how best to boost natural light when the days shorten. Any lighting scheme you install should be designed for daytime winter use as well as the obvious nocturnal one. Mini spots and flexible fibre optic lighting are both excellent ways of introducing illumination and interest to a room – an additional layer of light that has both a functional and a decorative purpose.

If you design with the seasons in mind, you might also think about how to keep floors cool underfoot in summer and warm in winter. A simple way of doing this is to lay two layers of flooring: something solid, such as wood or stone, over which rugs or matting can be placed. Changes in temperature can then be reflected effortlessly by removing or replacing the top layer.

You should also think about how you use a room in winter as opposed to summer. You might want to position furniture slightly differently, perhaps drawing seating closer together for a more intimate mood. Warmer months are often synonymous with living half inside and half in the garden. Open doors and windows extend the feeling of space, so interiors become airier than in winter. If you keep major pieces of furniture, such as sofas and beds, fairly neutral it is then possible to transform them completely according to the season through textured items such as cushions and runners. Winter might be signified by red velvet runners on the table, a mohair throw on the bed or charcoal felt cushions on the sofa. In summer, white satin runners, plain linen sheets and cashmere cushions might be the order of the day. Think about investing in some items that can be used all year round, such as reversible throws in two contrasting fabrics.

Smaller, more portable pieces of furniture offer an additional way of recognising seasonal differences. Transparent or semi-transparent materials, such as glass, Perspex or burnished metal, reflect light and make an ideal addition to summer rooms. Winter might call for more solidity and stronger colour, so wood or lacquer may be a better choice. Tables or occasional chairs that can be exchanged according to season are just as important as smaller accessories, such as vases or fruit bowls.

Flowers are the ideal way of reflecting changes in the seasons, as well as being one of the easiest ways to inject colour. Think of the fiery red of autumn dahlias as opposed to the pure white of summer lilies, for example. They are also a way of bringing scent into a home and scent, like colours and textures, should always be in tune with the seasons. But flowers are not the only way of introducing nature into the home: simple arrangements, such as winter twigs in white sand, can provide equally pleasing focal points.

Finally, build up a collection of objects that you love for their decorative qualities. Consciously divide these into winter or summer displays. Pack them away until the right time of year, so that you are continually changing the small items in a room as well as the large ones. This will prevent the interior from becoming static and you will enjoy rediscovering them anew every six months or so.

ABOVE Crisp white linen sheets and pillowcases create ripples against a bedhead upholstered in creamy ostrich leather. The luxuriant qualities of the latter set the signature of the room, but other textures can be changed according to season or mood.

OPPOSITE Ostrich leather has also been chosen for the elegant Roman blind in the same bedroom. A sheer curtain has been hung in front, which contrasts in both texture and the direction of stripes.

PAGE 66 A shelf unit of leather and wood has a back panel of lit milk glass, which creates an evocative backdrop to silhouettes of coral in a bronze pot. The simplicity of the arrangement allows the filigree-fine texture of the coral to be appreciated fully.

PAGE 67 Textured silver wallpaper and a Perspex box of white sand evoke a wintry setting for bleached dogwood twigs gathered from the garden.

OPPOSITE Ivory-coloured dahlias make a dramatic centrepiece when gathered into a large Perspex box – the perfect addition to an airy summer scheme.

PAGE 70 The concrete bed base and concrete floor are given textural definition here by the addition of a white satin runner.

PAGE 71 Viewed here through a Perspex panel, it is possible to see how each component – from the concrete base and ostrich bedhead to the white dahlias and Perspex furniture – combines to create a room that is cool, calm and considered.

ABOVE LEFT Kelly Hoppen fabric in a variety of stripes has been used here to cover the bedhead, duvet cover and pillowcases in soft taupes and creams.

ABOVE RIGHT A floating shelf makes an almost invisible backdrop for identical glass vases, each holding a single-stem cream Bianca rose. Submerging the buds in this way accentuates the contemporary look.

OPPOSITE The floor and walls of this wet room are limestone, which is not only practical but brings natural beauty to the room.

PAGE 76 Mohair and fake polar bear throws on a cotton chenille bedspread are carefully folded to create a quiet still life. The small cushions are linen in envelopes of sheer.

PAGE 77 Unlined linen curtains fall to the floor, creating waves of light and dark against a plain wool carpet.

ABOVE LEFT Broad bands of alternative-coloured fabric on cushions and curtains accentuate the linear design of this harmonious room. Here the vertical of one plays against the horizontal of the other to interesting effect. Textural contrast is apparent in the use of cashmere wool against suede and calico. Even the way the fabric falls sends out ripples against the floor.

ABOVE RIGHT Cushions do not have to relate to function, but can be used visually to layer a look. These comprise a combination of satin and chenille and look so delicious they are almost edible. Stacked on a velour-covered ottoman, they add height to this corner of the room, so balancing out other elements of the scheme. When the ottoman is in use, the cushions can be put aside.

ABOVE LEFT The surface of a wall can be left undecorated without remaining blank. Here a pitted plaster-effect paint finish introduces texture for beauty and interest. Increasingly, surfaces such as this are designed to be inviting to the fingers as well as to the eyes. By hanging something of a contrasting texture, such as the silk and linen of these curtains, this effect is emphasised.

ABOVE RIGHT Much is made in decorating texts of the importance of light within a room. However, shadow can be just as mood-enhancing. The reading lamp here is positioned to throw light onto the crewelwork upholstery, but it also casts a half light upon the clay figure standing on the wenge radiator case, etching it against the surface of the wall to dramatic effect.

STILL-LIFE COMPOSITIONS

Central to the enjoyment of a room is visual comfort – it must please the eye in order for the body and mind to relax. I give just as much attention to the way cushions are stacked or flowers are arranged as I do to wall treatments or styles of furniture. For me, the effect of a beautifully designed scheme would be ruined if there were even the smallest note of disharmony. Still-life compositions are not just about the obvious, such as how a coffee table might be arranged. They are about paying attention to every vista in a space.

Think first about what you see when you first walk into a particular room. Do you have the opportunity to introduce a focal point of some description, perhaps one fabulous piece of furniture or eye-catching work of art? There is no point having a centrepiece like this unless you are going to lavish attention on it, so consider its height, shape, colour and texture. Now look for ways of making the most of these, perhaps by installing display lighting or repositioning other furniture so that it stands in a space of its own. The strength of a focal point is that it should need very little else surrounding it, so be disciplined and reduce the number of objects in the room, rather than adding more.

Because focal points are so integral to a room, it is hard to decorate first and then find one that fits exactly in terms of size, subject and style. If when you are thinking about the space and how you are going to position the furniture, you can see in your mind's eye the place for something dramatic, then carry this image around with you until you find what you are looking for. It should be something you love; a can't-live-without buy from which the rest of the scheme will evolve.

Although the first view of a room is important, it is necessary to consider other angles, too. Walk around the room, stand and sit, think about how the dynamics of the space change according to where you are. How are you going to arrange objects so that you magnify the strong points of the room while diminishing the weak ones? If, for example, you have your back turned to your chosen focal point when sitting on the sofa, how are you going to create a secondary tableau to provide interest? As you are now at a different eye level, you will have to design something that corresponds with this – perhaps a collection of some sort arranged on a table or pictures that are stacked against a wall rather than hung.

Take time to think honestly about the objects themselves. Too often we hang on to things out of habit, nostalgia or laziness. We become so accustomed to seeing certain items every day that in fact we no longer see them at all. Yet why bother to give room in your life to anything you don't absolutely love? Absence makes the heart grow fonder, so if in doubt pack all the extraneous things away and spend time enjoying your totally blank canvas. If after a month you can barely remember what used to be in a certain place, then it is probably time to say goodbye to it for good. Only those items you consciously miss should be put back again.

Remember that there are essentially two reasons for buying objects for the home. The first is because they mean something. If you travel a lot, for example, you may enjoy collecting souvenirs – often beautiful, hand-crafted objects – that remind you of certain locations and occasions. In other words, you are buying for the object itself – not with any decorative scheme in mind. The second way of buying is to decide on a theme, such as a particular colour or material, and to make this a pivotal factor in your scheme. It means that shopping trips take on more purpose, as you will be looking for specific shapes, colours or styles that complement everything else.

There is no right or wrong here, because homes are intensely personal places. However, it is worth recognising which category you fit and deciding how comfortable you are with that. The first injects a home with character and individuality; the second achieves a more cohesive, visual effect. Perhaps it is enough to say that you should at least be confident that everything you buy fits into one of those definitions.

Next, you have to think about how you are going to arrange these objects for the greatest visual impact. If you have identical or similar objects, group these close together so that they become more than the sum of their parts. Decide whether you want a symmetrical or asymmetrical grouping, or whether you are going to include other objects that relate in some way – perhaps through height, form, colour or texture.

Remember the importance of contrast: an arrangement of highly decorative objects will be best appreciated when set against a backdrop of clean, straight lines. A quiet scheme of creams and taupes might benefit from a jolt of red. A narrow alcove might suggest the proportions of a small painting, so instead fill it with the biggest mirror you can.

Finally, take time over detailing. Your friends and family might think you are mad to spend hours grouping arrangements of objects or paintings, only to do it again a day later, but the perfectionist in you is a thing to celebrate. Folding, stacking and ensuring everything is in alignment are the hallmarks of the unashamed idealist.

OPPOSITE A pair of pomelos recreate the beauty of an old master painting. Their waxy skin and vibrant colour have been highlighted here by carefully considered lighting which brings out their texture to perfection. The wenge tray on which they stand merges quietly into the background.

ABOVE A room should comprise many pleasing views, both large and small. This floating shelf is the setting for a contemplative still life, which combines striking black-and-white photography with antique silver boxes, carefully stacked, and a Perspex box of iris leaves. Each object is carefully aligned with the next to achieve Zen-like harmony.

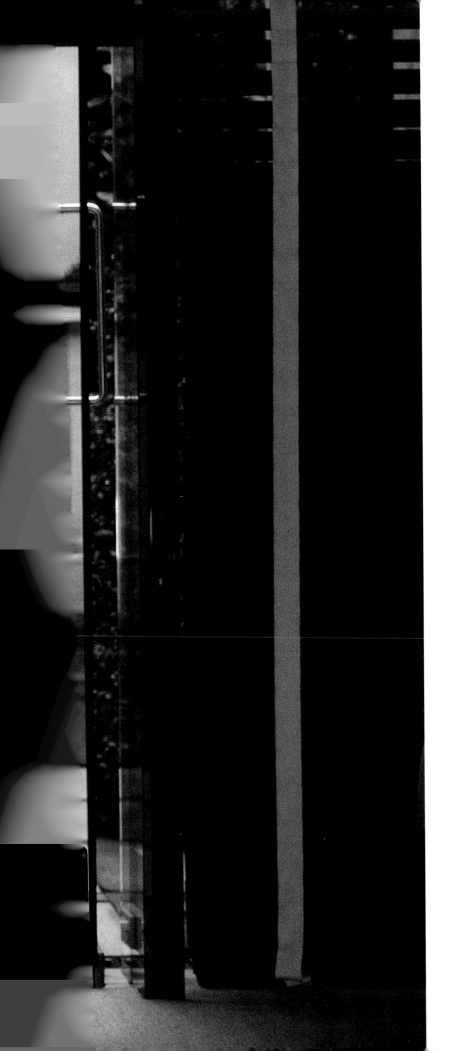

Scenes within a room can be arranged for maximum visual impact. If you have an object that is bold in scale, form or colour, use it as the eye-catching centrepiece of a room. Here, a magnificent bronze head of a horse has been cleverly positioned to create a focal point within this elegant living room, although in fact it is located in the courtyard outside. Commissioning a pedestal of the right height and material is essential to the success of such a piece. The wenge slatted blinds create a dramatic frame around it, adding to the sense of grandeur. These have pale cotton binding tape running down their length, accentuating the lines within the room and forcing the eye forwards. Lush greenery on topiary plants in front of the statue and trees behind accentuate the depth of vision. Furniture within the room has also been positioned so as to lead the eye forwards, as with the centrally placed wenge table on which a simple glass bowl of pussy willow and arum lilies is equivalent to visual punctuation. The result is a spectacular tableau built around one strong image.

OPPOSITE The smallest of details are relevant to the success of a scheme. Here, exquisite stitching on a leather chair introduces a further layer of texture and pattern.

ABOVE Walls of shelving can be used as striking display areas. Here, the central shelf has been designed to accommodate the television, because often it is better to be bold where home leisure equipment is concerned rather than attempt to conceal it. Other shelves hold books, stacked aesthetically rather than in conventional rows. Interspersed with these are decorative objects. Stacking black-and-white photography at floor level has the effect of drawing the eye downwards from the television towards the more unusual forms of the head rests. Fibre optic lighting has been inset into shelf edges, adding a witty touch to an otherwise wholly functional piece of furniture.

OPPOSITE Kitchens are often an unexpected source of objects that are decorative as well as functional. These humble glass mixing bowls have been half filled with white sand on which white cattleya orchids lie. The marble table on which they stand makes a visual link to the marble fireplace behind, between which stands a white leather Mies van der Rohe stool with cashmere throw.

ABOVE A white lacquer tray makes the perfect home for miniature water bottles. The table on which they stand is wenge, with a stainless steel insert running down the centre that complements the white metal Venetian blinds at the window.

ABOVE The vertical lines of this taupe-painted cupboard have been intersected by the wooden floor and leather-covered stool, stressing the graphic qualities of the scheme. Inset glass shelves cut out of one panel make the perfect display area for a collection of white ceramic bottles – another example of how very modest objects can be used to decorative effect. The result is calm, harmonious and soothing to the eye.

PAGE 90 A stack of white towels on a wenge slatted shelf makes an interesting textural play against a limestone floor. By storing them at a lower height than is usual, they become part of a pleasing still-life composition.

PAGE 91 The interior of this bathroom cupboard has been lit to create an unexpected display area. A line of empty bottles etched across this backdrop looks beautiful in its simplicity, but the shelf can also be used for more practical purposes.

Walls are often underestimated in design, seen only as boundaries between one area and another. However, they are also backdrops to items – both functional and decorative – and can be used to layer up interest. The limestone wall and work surface of this bathroom are not only quietly beautiful, but also inviting to the touch and immensely durable. The lines of the shaving mirror create a strong form against this neutral canvas.

ABOVE The curve of a television screen cuts across the outline of the skylight above, creating an intriguing sequence of lines and arcs.

BELOW The side view of a cotton-covered chair with vertically stacked cushions shows a similar effect of rounded edges intersecting the lines of the linen curtains. Horizontal banding at the bottom adds a further visual twist.

OPPOSITE Bathrooms are often overlooked in terms of creating aesthetically pleasing scenes, but this limestone design is used as the backdrop for a fabulous combination of objects. The seductive curve of the 1960s Panton chair in fibreglass makes an unexpected setting for a still life of vellum books and ivory boxes. The colour and texture of the vellum are picked up in the taupe-coloured towels on the rail behind.

ABOVE AND OPPOSITE Cushions are the ideal way of combining textures for contrast. These carefully stacked examples are made of leather with velvet, leather with voile or simple cotton, complementing the ostrich bedhead and sheer curtains perfectly.

PAGES 98 AND 99 The way in which each element in a space relates to all the others is key to the visual success of a room. The Zen-like atmosphere of this calm living room is evident not only through pale colours, but also through the way shapes are echoed from the black-and-white photographs of roses, to the linen seats below, to the two-by-three arrangement of roses in glass bowls on the table. A bird's-eye view of these shows pussy willow twisted around the circumference with a rose head placed centrally.

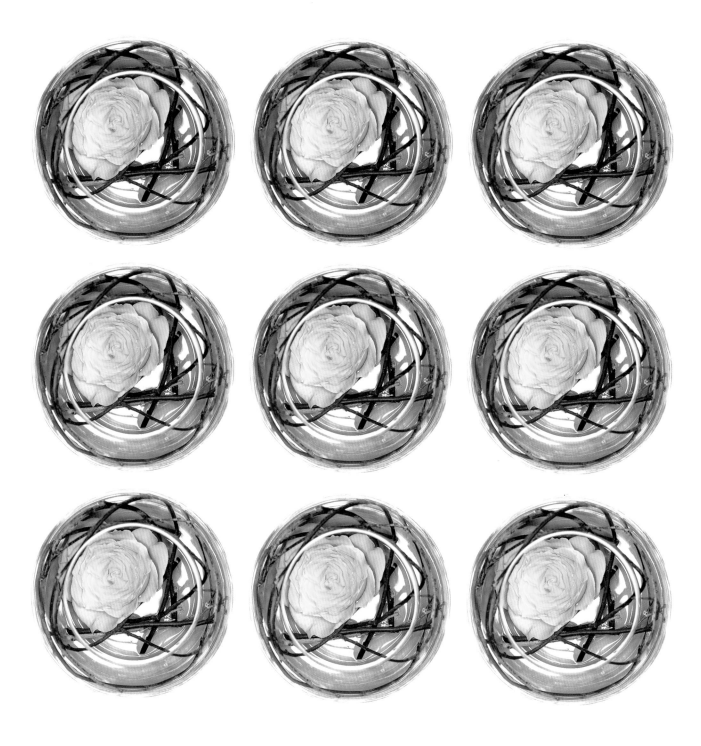

REFLECTIONS AND ECHOES

What I strive for above all else when decorating is absolute harmony. An interior should not be made up of a series of disparate elements, but should consist of carefully considered ideas that vibrate throughout each room. Rooms may have different characters that accentuate their separateness or alternatively melt into each other, so continuing this feeling of reverberation. At its best, an entire house will be visually in tune on every level from basement to attic.

The reflections and echoes of a room are a way of achieving this harmony. However, reflections have three interpretations for the decorator, each of them contributing to the overall design of a room. The first is literal: the idea of introducing reflective surfaces that then magnify an effect. Mirrors are the most obvious way of doing this, but they are not the only option. There are now wallpaper and paint finishes that have reflective qualities as well as textural ones. Metallic papers, for example, not only create interest on a wall, but when combined with good lighting and interesting objects create the most beautiful and subtle reflections and shadows throughout the space.

Glossy surfaces also bring added interest to a room. Juxtapose them with a contrasting matt texture, so highlighting their individual qualities. A stainless steel runner down a wenge table is a striking example of how a reflective surface interplays with a dense one, as is a satin band around a velvet cushion. Glass furniture or accessories are the most obvious ways to introduce a reflective surface to a scheme, but consider mixing plain with opaque or etched glass for a more contemporary look.

The second interpretation is more intellectual: the idea of reflecting on a room and its success from a design point of view. It is about taking time to think carefully about what has been created and whether there are improvements still to be made. So often people make a good job of transforming a room decoratively, but then fail to put in the last five per cent of work – the detailing. Finishing off a room well is one of the hardest tasks, yet it really does make the difference between something that looks amateur and a professional result. Be critical: try to take the vantage point of someone walking in for the first time. Pause to contemplate whether you have achieved everything you wanted to in the space.

The third interpretation is about sending out reflections through a room, metaphorically speaking, and this is closely related to the idea of harmony. It centres on the idea that colours, textures, forms and lines should all work together in perfect balance. It means that there should be a reason for everything that has been chosen and where it has been placed. You must train your eye to focus on what is there and make confident decisions about what works and what does not. A scheme might appear very simple – neutral colours, clean lines – but that might disguise the care that has been taken to make sure everything is in perfect alignment. The line of a rug, for example, might reflect that of a banquette. A row of ceramic bowls on a mantelpiece might link subtly to a collection of match strikers on a cabinet. This ability to analyse shape, scale and line – and to play on it – is integral to the way I decorate.

Having thought about reflections, now consider echoes. The echoes of a room are the subliminal messages that certain objects, fabrics, furniture shapes or colours send out. You might, for example, bring nature into your scheme by including organic objects or simple arrangements of leaves, twigs and flowers. You might suggest the ocean through a colour scheme or bowls of pebbles. You might inject a note of glamour from the past with swathes of Fortuny fabric or black-and-white photographic images. This is a very subtle level of decorating, but can be the way of designing something really special. Suggestion is a powerful force, so remember that understatement is the key. One perfectly placed object is enough, so don't feel tempted to overdo it. Gone are the days of heavily themed rooms: the contemporary approach to decorating demands a more restrained approach.

Start by making the space as pure and uncluttered as possible. Now take one object you really love, something with eye-catching form. Place it where it can be seen to best effect, but now really observe its shape and lines. Is there a way of repeating these in some way? It might be that you have chosen to position it against the window, in which case a curtain or blind may offer the potential to make a visual link. Or perhaps you can find something of a similar style, but on a much smaller scale. If so, is there a way of arranging this object nearby, on a mantelpiece or side table perhaps? Once you have your starting point, it should be possible to build on it.

Finally, make sure you maintain this disciplined frame of mind in your approach to the whole room. Do not introduce other items that stop the flow from object to object. Remember that all these gentle visual links are a way of achieving a cohesive whole.

When choosing furniture that will be used on an everyday basis, such as seating, remember that comfort must be high on your list of priorities. As far as design is concerned, it is best to opt for something that has pleasing form and offers some flexibility – a sense of timelessness is also an advantage. These graceful dining chairs are covered in simple calico, which suits their clean lines and painted frames perfectly. However, they can also be transformed with the use of simple slip covers that pull over the top, creating an entirely different look according to mood, season or occasion.

LEFT AND BELOW The milky blues and slate greys of this beautifully dressed table create a scene as cool as winter. Mirrors are the conventional companion to fireplaces, but here textured silver wallpaper makes an interesting alternative while still introducing a reflective quality. Organic shapes, such as the collection of coral and the swathes of pleated table linen, make a visual play against the underlying structure found in rows of ceramic eggs and boxes of upright twigs. A scrim runner over the calico cloth emphasises the sense of order.

OPPOSITE Consider how each item in a room relates to the shapes and textures around it. Here, the intricate surface of a shagreen console has been echoed in a collection of beads displayed in a silvered glass bowl. The blues, greys and greens of the composition are reminiscent of the sea, so that at first glance the beads resemble shells and pebbles gathered from the shore.

ABOVE Pearl buttons displayed on a white lacquer tray catch light and colour, as though they were bubbles in water. Conventionally used to embellish other objects, here they have been arranged in isolation so that their own beauty can be fully appreciated.

A close-up of the view shown on page 104 throws the spotlight onto the fabulous wealth of textures. The organic form of coral is so strong that very little of it is needed to have an impact within a room. Here its sculptural qualities have been accentuated by the uneven surface of the silver wallpaper and the smoothness of the marble fireplace. The black-and-white image behind echoes the sensuous shape of the coral arms.

Roses have been synonymous with beauty for centuries. Here they have been given a contemporary twist by submerging them in Perspex vases rather than displaying them – as is traditional – long-stemmed and tall. The trick of producing such an effect for yourself is to cut the roses very short and place them in the vase before adding water. Trickle it in slowly and stop the moment the rose begins to move, otherwise it will not sit perfectly. Seen in this way, it is as if they are framed, frozen in time and space. Note too how displaying the roses individually encourages one to focus on their individual characteristics. Their creamy colour and silky texture needs no other accompaniment.

ABOVE The reflective surfaces of a row of silver teapots highlights them in a room dominated by wenge furniture.

OPPOSITE A trio of floating shelves underlit with fibre optic lighting creates a calm, contemplative focal point in this restrained living room. The creamy leather upholstery and bolster cushion of the modern *chaise-longue* blend with the other subdued colours.

BELOW The interiors of drawers and cupboards should be as carefully considered as the exterior.

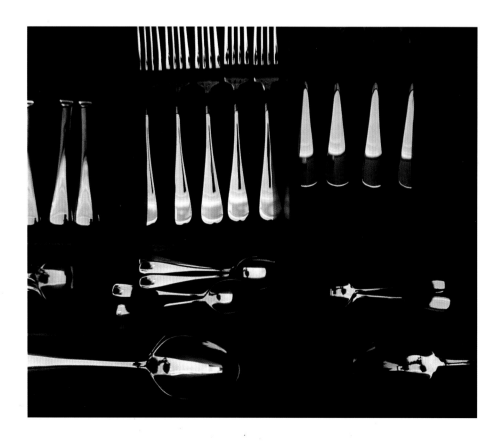

The addition of one material into a scheme can greatly influence the overall style or mood. Wood, for example, might be regarded as too traditional a choice for furniture, but can be introduced through artefacts that reveal its textural beauty. This collection of African head rests creates wonderful sculptural shapes against the taupe-painted wall. Floating shelves have been chosen because they are unobtrusive and do not detract from what is displayed on them. The richness of the wood contrasts perfectly with the contemporary elegance of the slim silvered glass light. This combination is a perfect example of how antique objects can be juxtaposed with modern ones to powerful effect.

OPPOSITE Candles are a decorating essential, not just because they cast such a soft light but because they are also a way of introducing scent. A sculpted candle looks fabulous when seen up close next to a waxy palm leaf.

ABOVE A collection of freeform glass vases inspired by the shapes of pebbles brings robust form, ripples of colour and reflective texture to this otherwise tranquil living room. Propped on floating shelves above is a group of white-framed photographs depicting roses. The organic shapes of the glass contrast in an interesting way with this linear arrangement.

OPPOSITE In this wenge-and-limestone bathroom a gloriously textured wooden artefact creates an effective focal point.

ABOVE A textured wall and wenge dado provide the backdrop for a linen-covered bedhead and bedspread. Silk cushions inject opulence into the scheme, while a row of dark blue hyacinth bulbs on a bed of shingle placed on the wenge table introduce a flash of colour.

BELOW Two huge glass vases in which Liberty amaryllis are submerged echo the lines of ceiling-to-floor panels in the background.

PAGE 120 Track lighting has been inset into this ceiling, making it possible to achieve some spectacular lighting effects.

PAGE 121 A pebble floor is a fabulous way of creating contrast and making texture central to a decorative scheme.

LAYERS OF MOOD

The world is an increasingly frantic place. As cities expand, it seems that personal space contracts. The square metres we call our own are ever more precious: the physical buffer between stress and sanity.

All of this makes me very aware when designing a room that it must not only look and feel fabulous, but must also reflect the changing moods of the people who live there. When you walk into your home after another wearying day, you want to feel caressed and soothed within seconds. But when you wake to greet a new morning, you need to feel energised and invigorated.

Atmosphere is not something you can inject into a scheme from the word go. It needs to be layered on through many different elements. You need to start by asking yourself how you want to use a particular space and how you want to feel when you are in it. It could be, for example, that you rarely have time to unwind except in the evening. Therefore a nocturnal decorative scheme could be more appropriate than a diurnal one. It might be that you are more likely to eat out with friends than to entertain at home, in which case an intimate table for two will suffice instead of a full-size dining table. In other words, break away from convention and make decisions that suit the way you live.

The most powerful mood-enhancing ingredient is light. I have already talked about the importance of understanding natural light (Spaces Seen and Unseen), but artificial lighting is crucial when it comes to influencing atmosphere. If you can afford it, employ the services of a lighting specialist. You will be amazed at how the right fittings can transform an interior. Put simply, there are three lighting layers. The first, task lighting, is about fulfilling practical considerations: having a light to shave by, chop vegetables under, read in bed, and so on. The second, atmospheric lighting, is about controlling the mood of a room – creating pockets of light throughout an interior that highlight certain features and draw you into a home. When you walk in from the cold night air, for example, you don't want to find yourself blinking from over-bright lights. The feeling of home being a safe sanctuary is best engendered by lights that calm and soothe. Finally, lighting has become such an exciting field for new design that you may consider a third layer: sculptural lighting. These are individual pieces that not only illuminate, but also decorate a room. They can be bought instead of paintings, because they are the equivalent of three-dimensional art. Taking many different forms and sizes, they are often the ideal focal point in a contemporary setting.

However, lighting is only the beginning. Next you must think about what you are going to illuminate and how you can make that a decorative feature of the room. Colour and texture, for example, take on new depth when lit well. Consider colour first. Although I enjoy working with a palette that verges on the monochrome, I also love to use jolts of colour for visual impact. Red is fabulous because you need so little of it to create something exciting. It might be just a red vase, a tray of red carnations or a chair upholstered in red chenille with a contrasting cream suede cushion. Burnt oranges, voluptuous purples and earthy greens can also make neutrals vibrate. Interestingly, blues are less easy, often appearing too insipid when placed against the rich taupes, charcoals and oatmeals that inspire my use of colour.

Texture underpins all my designs. Fabrics are my starting point for each room, so the mix of cashmere, leather, linen, mohair, wool, satin, cotton, velvet, taffeta and others is pivotal not only to the look of a scheme, but also to its atmosphere. When combined with the other materials in a room – stainless steel, wenge, glass, plaster, vellum, limestone and so on – that character becomes even more firmly imprinted.

However, this is not quite the end of the story. If a house or apartment is to continue to delight, it must feed the senses. You might think that the eye is the first to respond when entering a room. In fact, it is the nose. A home must always smell right. Fresh flowers are the obvious way of achieving this, but there are also wonderful scented candles to choose from, incense burners or oils for lamp rings. Freshly baked bread or freshly brewed coffee is also synonymous with a feeling of well being, so let free the home-maker in you. Have scents in every room that are appropriate to their use. Our ears are also far more responsive than we think. Music playing gently in the background can lift the spirits after a hard day, so consider installing a timer on your sound system that will allow you to hear a favourite album before the key is even in the lock. How a room feels is fundamental to its success, so choose textural combinations that will envelop you and make you feel secure and cocooned. Enjoy running fingers over fabrics that are inviting to the senses.

Finally, it is true that a room must be visually harmonious if you are going to relax fully. It is not enough just to decorate it the way you want: you must maintain that look. Make time each morning to tidy up before you go to work: that way you know it will always be a pleasure to come back to, and will reward the effort you make ten times over.

This simply decorated living room brings together many key design strategies. The textured wall, for example, incorporates a runner effect which stresses the underlying grid structure of the space. The roughness of this juxtaposed with the smoothness of adjacent flat-painted walls is interesting both to the eye and to the touch. The monochrome scheme combines a dark wenge floor and table and simple linen upholstery, with only the sharp green of cocoa leaves to inject vivid colour into the room. Contrast is evident not only in textural choices – such as the sheer curtains and wooden artefact – but in the way that such a traditional fireplace has been dressed in a contemporary look, with a trio of small ceramic bowls and silver beakers placed at each end of the mantelpiece. A group of three Perspex pots on the table echoes these arrangements. The expressive curve of the leaf is striking against the order apparent elsewhere.

ABOVE The stainless steel runner inlaid down this wenge table is a
natural backdrop for glass vases filled with green variegated
leaves. Submerging them in this way makes it possible to
appreciate fully their lacy texture and glorious colour. White
milophapos orchids resting on a wreath of pussy willow complete
the picture.

OPPOSITE A close-up of the cocoa leaf seen on the mantelpiece on
page 125 shows the interplay between its waxy stripes and the
roughness of the textured wall.

PAGE 128 A petal-shaped silver bowl on a wenge table makes a
fabulous display vessel for mother-of-pearl buttons. The amount
of light each surface attracts contributes to the dramatic effect.

PAGE 129 Lights set into the skirting height of a bathroom
accentuate the atmosphere of this textured surface.

OPPOSITE One strong material is enough to set the atmospheric tone of a room. This guest bathroom has a carved slate basin and specialist-effect painted walls. The density of these has been balanced with a wenge-framed mirror. On the slate worktop is a Perspex box filled with shingle and hyacinth bulbs, which again bring together the qualities of matt and gloss.

ABOVE The base of a wenge-framed mirror is seen set against a painted radiator cover on which stand three horn beakers. These not only introduce a textural dimension, but also inject pattern into the scheme.

ABOVE Think laterally when considering how natural objects might be displayed within a room. Here a wenge box has been packed with snake grass to spectacular effect. The wenge table and linen curtains provide a neutral canvas for the arrangement.

OPPOSITE Sticks of bamboo have been tied together here to create a decorative frame for a ceramic plate. The granite surface and textured wall make an ideal base for the reflective surfaces of the glass under plate, side plate and coaster.

PAGE 134 Even natural objects can be embellished for interest. Here artichokes have been wrapped in coir string to increase their textural significance. A simple lacquer bowl is the perfect foil for such elaborate leaves.

PAGE 135 Back-lit floating shelves above the slate work surface of a city kitchen are used as a display area for a row of identical white ceramic bowls. Three moss balls above make an eye-catching focal point, while baking trays of greenery continue the colour theme.

OPPOSITE An intimate dining area has been created here by using linen panels to separate off one corner of a room. The wenge table and chairs are extra high, stressing the vertical lines of the room. These are further accentuated by the tall lamp and the gold runners that fall to the floor on each side. Horizontal widths of bark balance the proportions of the space and make interesting vessels for food.

ABOVE The space between this wenge radiator cover and the wenge mirror frame makes an ideal backdrop for a row of glass vases. Orchids wrapped in leaves have a Japanese-style beauty on which the eye can rest.

ABOVE The concertina action of this antique chain mirror sets up a sequence of fabulous reflections in this entrance hall, fooling the eye into believing the space is bigger than it is. Plain woollen upholstery has been teamed with a magnificent devore cushion, while an industrial wall light has been juxtaposed with an ornate glass-based one. The shagreen table, inlaid chinoiserie boxes and Chinese trunk accentuate the mood of restrained opulence.

OPPOSITE A wenge light with linen shade casts dramatic lighting over a chair upholstered in Alcantara suede with matching cushions.

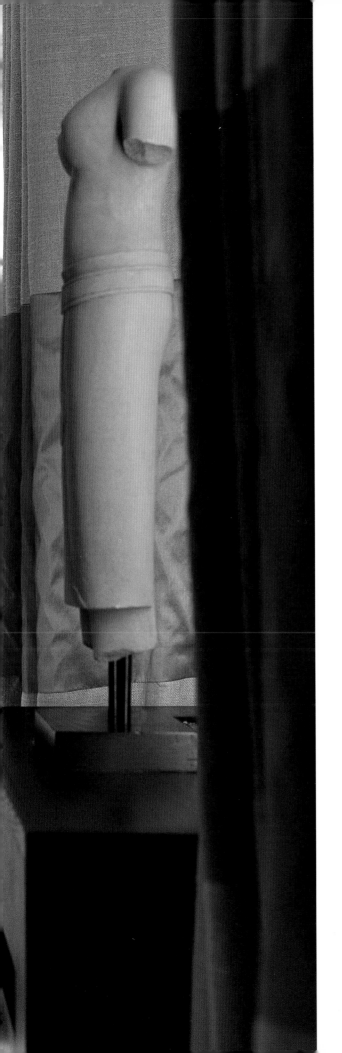

LEFT A quiet corner for reading has been created in this elegant bedroom, with a lamp carefully positioned over a crewelwork chair. Wenge-and-mirror cupboards across the width of the room increase the feeling of space, while horizontal bands on the linen curtains also accentuate the proportions of the room. An antiquarian clay figure on a wenge radiator cover is positioned for maximum visual impact.

BELOW Sheer curtains and linen Roman blinds have been used together here to create interesting effects of light and shadow. These have been emphasised by placing a semi-translucent philodendron leaf in a Perspex box against the window. Its luminous finish contrasts with the wenge desk on which the only other object is a pencil pot.

STRUCTURE AND FREEDOM

Those who are familiar with my work know how important the idea of structure is to me. I have already explained how I design in a very linear way, seeing each room as a grid system into which every component must be placed. However, the hardest part of design lies in achieving a room that is thought out down to the last detail, but does not appear to be formal or over-structured. Your home should make you feel very comfortable and relaxed, rather than leave you perching on the edge of a chair worrying about putting anything out of place. Therefore structure must be used in tandem with freedom, a sense of liberation that imbues every level of design.

Freedom can have many interpretations. It can relate, for example, to form. Think of the hardness of linear form, but now imagine ways to soften this: organic shapes, for instance, effectively break up a design that is very stark. This is one of the reasons why I love to use flowers, foliage, rocks, shells and fruit in my work. Not only do they bring qualities such as colour and scent to a scheme, but they are the perfect way of blurring the sharper edges of an interior.

These organic forms have become a powerful influence in design in recent years. Furniture and lighting designers have looked to the natural world for many of the shapes now found at the cutting edge of design. Curves used in conjunction with lines bring sensuality to a space, perhaps because gentle undulations are so rooted in our minds to the female form. They can be used in small proportions within a scheme and still have an impact. Bowls, vases and dishes are just a few examples of how you might introduce a curvaceous layer. Or you could use a larger item, such as a chair, to draw the eye. I find it enormously satisfying to take something like the curve of a steel day bed and place it against the vertical line of a blind or wall-hung runner. The way that one object cuts across another creates a visual jolt of excitement.

One word of warning, though: I may put things in to shock the eye, but they do have to work. You can't just throw something in for the sake of it. I have seen designs that should look fantastic because all the individual ideas are good, but somehow they fail to work because they lack continuity. This is why it is so important to ensure that the core structure of a room is correct before looking for ways to free it up. Structure gives a scheme a cohesive whole, be it through colour, texture or form, so this must be absolutely right if other ideas are also to work.

Design demands a touch of courage though, so better to try something unexpected and for it not to work than not to try at all. What matters is being self-critical enough to distinguish between the two. After all, freedom is also about harnessing lateral thinking to interesting effect. Because I am known for using luxurious fabrics in rooms, such as leather, cashmere, taffeta and silk, people assume that everything must be expensive. Nothing could be further from the truth. I also use felt, scrim, towelling and cotton if I think they feel and look right. In fact I take an egalitarian view, not distinguishing between the opulent and the modest. What counts is the dance they make together.

Also, I love to use the humblest household object in a totally different way – a baking tray filled with moss balls perhaps, or Perspex mixing bowls filled with white sand and orchids. Look around your own home for similar ideas. The trick is to see not what something is used for, but what it could be used for in a different setting. Defy convention by stepping out of the ordinary.

This ability to use existing objects, rather than continually shopping for new ones, allows you to keep a house evolving without spending a fortune. You might need to do little other than raid the kitchen when you want to imprint a new look onto a room. It comes back to the same idea of having a strong structure in place. This can continue unchanged for a number of years, but what you layer over the surface is a way of ringing the changes from season to season or day to day.

Finally, freedom is about freedom of expression: the idea that a home should be so closely related to one's own character that it becomes as individual as you are. While it is good to use books like this to trawl through for ideas, it is even better to carry them on a step further for your own satisfaction. That kind of freedom comes with confidence, and it too can be increased if the structure of a room is in place. After all, if you know that all the foundation fabrics and key pieces of furniture are in harmony, you are assured of a room that looks chic and elegant no matter what. This then allows you to look for ways of imprinting it with a style of your own making, be it through objects you choose to display, a collection you have built up over the years, or the paintings you hang on your walls. The more disciplined you are at the beginning of your redesign, the more freedom you can allow at the end.

OPPOSITE Concealed spaces should be thought about as carefully as those that are on display. The door of this mirrored bathroom cupboard has a square shape cut out of its panel through which a light shines.

ABOVE Floating shelves lit with fibre optic lighting create a chic display area in a calm living room. A row of identical glass bowls filled with pussy willow and rose heads holds the eye. The arc each bowl makes is in contrast to the rigid lines of the room.

ABOVE A painted slatted door has been used to screen off a television when not in use.

OPPOSITE ABOVE Traditional balustrades have been replaced here with ones made of glass. The lustrous surface of these makes an interesting interplay against the density of the wood. The way they catch the light also introduces an additional layer of beauty into the room.

OPPOSITE BELOW Here, linen panels have replaced conventional doors in a dressing room. A slim wenge table at the far end is the setting for a dramatic wooden artefact, while the wenge-and-linen stool can be used for seating or the folding of clothes.

OPPOSITE This vermilion-and-taupe curtain has been made out of two colourways in the same wool, joined together to form a horizontal band. The richness of the tones and the boldness of the stripe create a striking effect.

ABOVE Plain linen cushions have been embellished here with horizontal bands of scarlet shot silk. This treatment accentuates the linear structure of the room and is a way of introducing a touch of opulence to an otherwise restrained scheme.

BELOW A wenge cabinet with nickel handles makes the perfect foil for three antique match strikers. The shape of these is surprisingly modern and sets up interesting contrasts of form and texture against the furniture.

ABOVE This breathtaking image shows a Perspex tray of crimson dahlias against a wenge table. It reveals that the simplest of arrangements can produce the most spectacular effects if only the imagination is harnessed effectively. Using flowers of a single colour in this way not only creates dramatic impact, but also throws the spotlight onto their individual shape and structure.

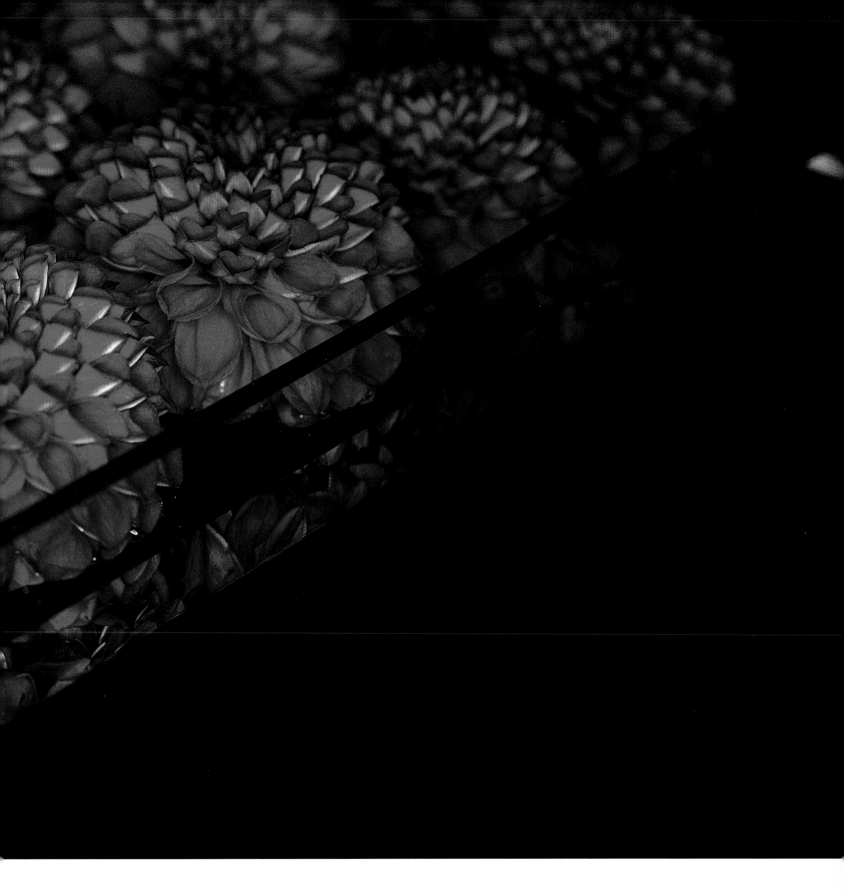

PAGE 150 A view through linen panels shows a different view of the bed seen on page 71. The concrete base and ostrich bedhead remain the same, but here a rich red velvet runner, charcoal-grey satin eiderdown and grey flannel cushions create a warmer mood .

PAGE 151 A close-up of the red velvet runner shows how it can also make a sensual base for plates of food.

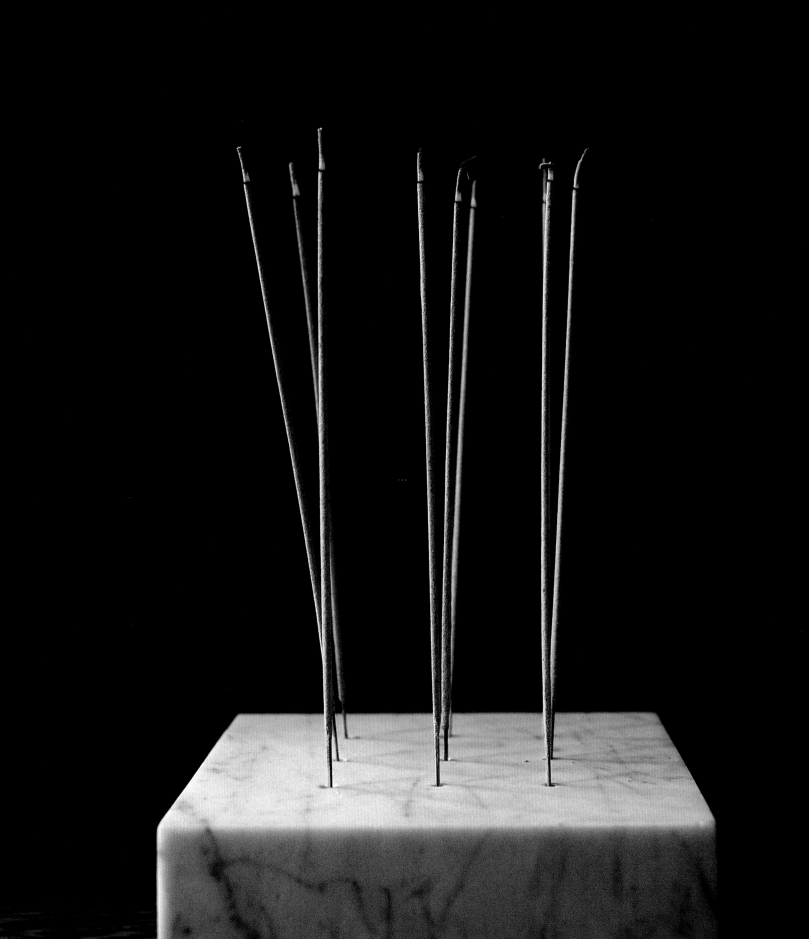

Now that scent has been recognised as a powerful influence on the ambience of a house, incense is no longer the domain of teenage bedrooms. Often stronger than candles or flowers, it is ideal for rooms where you want to create a warm, sensual atmosphere – particularly at night. Here a marble base has been used, which allows the incense sticks to become another linear ingredient of the scheme.

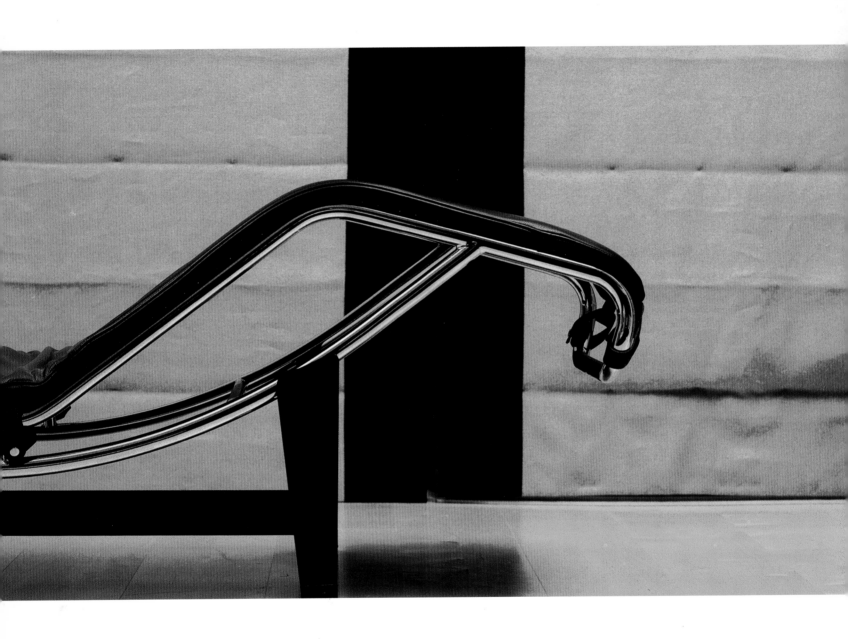

OPPOSITE The curve of a black leather-and-chrome *chaise* has been positioned to cut across the linear form of a linen Roman blind.
ABOVE A mushroom-shaped floor-standing light in metal.
BELOW A pair of Chinese chairs make an unexpected accompaniment to the graphic lines of a painted cupboard.

INDEX

AUTHOR'S ACKNOWLEDGEMENTS
Firstly, I would like to thank my clients who very kindly allowed me back into their homes to photograph the finished results; without their generous cooperation, this book would not have been possible. I would like to thank Melanie Rademacher and my entire team at Kelly Hoppen Interiors for making these projects run as smoothly as they do – Fran, Michelle, Ines, Belinda, Caroline, Lisa, Fabienne, Sarah, Christian, Michael, Richard, Stephanie, Ed, Kim and Alex. I could not achieve what I do without you!

ALSO A WARM THANK YOU TO:
John Carter for your extraordinary commitment, creativity and love for your work. Samantha Todhunter for your dedication and for understanding my work so well. You have been invaluable. Tom Stewart for your fantastic photography which has brought a whole new dimension to the way I see interiors through a lens. Helen Chislett for interpreting everything to perfection. It is pure pleasure working with you. Michelle Leach for running everything so beautifully. Anne, Mary and Jim for being such an impressive team and for making work a real joy. Alex because without you, none of this would ever happen.

KELLY HOPPEN PRODUCTS

FIRED EARTH
Two paint collections have been created – The Perfect Neutrals and Indochine. The Perfect Neutrals paint collection is a range of 16 specially mixed tones that form a neutral backdrop to any home. They are available in matt emulsion, acrylic eggshell, and some are available in oil gloss. The Indochine collection consists of bold striking colours that can be used to accentuate a space or even furniture. The colours are available in lacquer and matt emulsion finishes.

Head Office
Fired Earth
Twyford Mill
Oxford Road
Adderbury
OXON
OX17 3HP
Tel: 01295 812 088
Fax: 01295 810 832
www.firedearth.co.uk

SILENT GLISS
An all-encompassing collection of blinds, curtains and panels with co-ordinated cushions & throws. These are made from intricate and unique fabrics brought to life with a selection of eclectic design details, pulls and handles.

Head Office
Silent Gliss
Star Lane
Margate
Kent
CT9 4EF
Tel: 01843 863 571
Fax: 01843 864 503
info@silentgliss.co.uk

BOSANQUET IVES
Wall-to-wall fitted carpets are available in six neutral shades. This 100% wool carpet collection comes in 3 classic designs – trellis, basket ware and herringbone. The carpets are durable and natural, and work well with either traditional or contemporary settings.

Head Office
Bosanquet Ives
Imperial Studios
3–11 Imperial Road
London
SW6 2AG
Tel: 0207 384 7290
Fax: 0207 384 7299

KELATY
These four unique rug collections are made in Nepal by Tibetan weavers. Called Tibetan Tiger, Contemporary, Tribal and Transient, the designs are made from naturally dyed wool and silk. Each rug is a special piece of art that works equally on both floors and walls, and are available in all sizes.

Head Office
L Kelaty Ltd
Kelaty House
1st Way, Wembley
Middlesex
HA9 OJD
Tel: 0208 903 9998
Fax: 0208 903 5557

CLUB HOUSE ITALIA
A modern yet unusual furniture collection comprising of lighting and hard and soft furnishings. These pieces are created from a diverse range of materials, including wood, perspex and metal. A range of fabric is being developed to enhance the existing upholstery, cushions and throws.

Head Office
Club House Italia
Italy
Tel: 00 39 0543 791911
Fax: 00 39 0543 725244
clubhouse@clubhouseitalia.com

PUBLISHING DIRECTOR Anne Furniss

CREATIVE DIRECTOR Mary Evans

TEXT Helen Chislett

PHOTOGRAPHY Thomas Stewart

STYLING Samantha Todhunter

DESIGN Jim Smith

PRODUCTION Vincent Smith, Sarah Tucker

First published in 2001 by
Quadrille Publishing Limited
Alhambra House
27-31 Charing Cross Road
London WC2H OLS

Cataloguing in Publication Data:
A catalogue record for this book is available
from the British Library

ISBN 1 903845 14 9

Printed in Germany

PHOTOGRAPHIC ACKNOWLEDGEMENTS
The author and publisher would like to thank the following people and organizations for
lending items for photography. Page numbers indicate where to find the photographs in which
these items appear:

Aero (tel 020 7221 1950; 020 7351 0511) 95
Annick Richardson at Shanxi (tel 020 7498 7611) 138
Babylon (tel 020 7376 7255) 22,39,71,106,114,149
CA1 (tel 020 7611 5200) 149
C. Best (tel 020 7720 2306)104-105, 109
Ciancimino (tel 020 7730 9950) 33, 34,55,138
Coexistence (tel 020 7354 8817) 38
Bodo Sperlein (tel 020 7633 9413)105
David Champion (tel 020 7727 6016) 104-105, 114
Egg (tel 020 7235 9315) 135
Evertrading (tel 020 8878 4050) 76
Fired Earth (tel 01295 812 088) 38, 74, 114
General Trading Company (tel 020 7943 5303) 25, 48, 71, 92, 93, 116, 131
Guinevere (tel 020 7736 2917) 25, 32, 40, 54, 55, 71, 83 113
Habitat (tel 020 7255 2545) 88, 104-105
Hilary Batstone Antiques (tel 020 7730 5335) 138
Interiors Bis (tel 020 7838 1104) 59, 82, 113, 132
Jane Sacchi Linen (tel 020 7838 1001) 40, 68, 71, 150
Kate Hume Glass (tel 00 31 20 620 3030) 117
Kelaty (tel 020 8903 9998) 34
Michael Hoppen Gallery (tel 020 7352 3649) 14, 38, 60, 61, 83, 99, 113
Muji (tel 020 7436 1779) 1, 56, 63, 67, 71, 72, 83, 104-105, 110, 130, 113
Nom (tel 020 7584 4158) 12, 89, 104-105, 134
Pickett (tel 020 7823 5638) 58
RJ Norris Beds (tel 020 7274 5306) 71
Selfridges (tel 020 7629 1234) 53, 76
Silent Gliss (tel 01843 863571) 33, 71, 150
Space (tel 020 7229 6533) 39
The Cube (tel 020 7938 2244) 71, 152
Viaduct (tel 020 7278 8456) 99
William Yeoward (tel 020 7351 5454) 25
Wojnowski (tel 020 7584 5353) 99
Wolfin Textiles (tel 020 7636 4949) 102-103, 104-105
Yeoward South (tel 020 7498 4811) 12, 16, 44, 104-105, 118, 147
Yoma (tel 07957 881 926) 40, 150

Any queries, please call Samantha Todhunter on 020 7243 1065/m: 07818 042 900